Elements of Pronunciation

Intensive practice for intermediate and more advanced students

Colin Mortimer

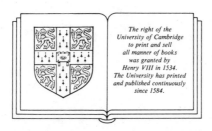

The right of the
University of Cambridge
to print and sell
all manner of books
was granted by
Henry VIII in 1534.
The University has printed
and published continuously
since 1584.

Cambridge University Press

Cambridge
New York   Port Chester
Sydney   Melbourne

Published by the Press Syndicate of the University of Cambridge
The Pitt Building, Trumpington Street, Cambridge CB2 1RP
40 West 20th Street, New York, NY 10011, USA
10 Stamford Road, Oakleigh, Melbourne 3166, Australia

© Cambridge University Press 1985

First published 1985
Sixth printing 1989

Printed in Great Britain
at the University Press, Cambridge

ISBN 0 521 26938 5 Book
ISBN 0 521 26334 4 Set of 4 cassettes

Publisher's note: This book has been compiled from a selection of the
dialogues previously published as five separate booklets by Colin
Mortimer: *Stress Time*, *Weak Forms*, *Clusters*, *Link-up* and
Contractions. The original recordings have been edited and paused to
make for easier use.

Drawings by Daria Gan (*Weak Forms*, *Clusters*, *Link-up* and
Contractions) and Peter Kneebone (*Stress Time*).

KY

Contents

Key to phonetic symbols

Vowels and diphthongs

iː	*as in*	see /siː/	ɜː	*as in*	fur /fɜː(r)/
ɪ	*as in*	sit /sɪt/	ə	*as in*	ago /əˈgəʊ/
e	*as in*	ten /ten/	eɪ	*as in*	page /peɪdʒ/
æ	*as in*	hat /hæt/	əʊ	*as in*	home /həʊm/
ɑː	*as in*	arm /ɑːm/	aɪ	*as in*	five /faɪv/
ɒ	*as in*	got /gɒt/	aʊ	*as in*	now /naʊ/
ɔː	*as in*	saw /sɔː/	ɔɪ	*as in*	join /dʒɔɪn/
ʊ	*as in*	put /pʊt/	ɪə	*as in*	near /nɪə(r)/
uː	*as in*	too /tuː/	eə	*as in*	hair /heə(r)/
ʌ	*as in*	cup /kʌp/	ʊə	*as in*	pure /pjʊə(r)/

Consonants

p	*as in*	pen /pen/	s	*as in*	so /səʊ/
b	*as in*	bad /bæd/	z	*as in*	zoo /zuː/
t	*as in*	tea /tiː/	ʃ	*as in*	she /ʃiː/
d	*as in*	did /dɪd/	ʒ	*as in*	vision /vɪʒn/
k	*as in*	cat /kæt/	h	*as in*	how /haʊ/
g	*as in*	get /get/	m	*as in*	man /mæn/
tʃ	*as in*	chin /tʃɪn/	n	*as in*	no /nəʊ/
dʒ	*as in*	June /dʒuːn/	ŋ	*as in*	sing /sɪŋ/
f	*as in*	fall /fɔːl/	l	*as in*	leg /leg/
v	*as in*	voice /vɔɪs/	r	*as in*	red /red/
θ	*as in*	thin /θɪn/	j	*as in*	yes /jes/
ð	*as in*	then /ðen/	w	*as in*	wet /wet/

To the student

Elements of Pronunciation can be used in class with a teacher, in a language laboratory with or without a teacher, or by a student working alone with a cassette recorder. If you are working alone either in a language laboratory or with a cassette recorder, you may like to follow this suggested procedure.

1. Play or read the complete dialogue and make sure you understand it. Some of the more difficult words are explained below the dialogue.
2. Play the recording, which is divided into three sections:
   - Phrases are picked out from the dialogue. You listen and repeat these until you feel confident about the particular pronunciation point which is being practised. The heading to the dialogue tells you what this is.
   - The dialogue is recorded without pauses. You may like to play this before you begin the pronunciation practice (see point 1 above). Listen now to the complete dialogue. You should make sure you understand it and can pick out the pronunciation point which is being practised. Play it as many times as you need.
   - The dialogue is then recorded with pauses so that you can repeat it in sections. Play it as many times as you need, repeating after the bleeps. Concentrate on the particular pronunciation point being practised, but make sure also that the overall pronunciation sounds natural.
3. Read the dialogue aloud without the recording. You may like to do this with a friend so that you can take a part each. Whether you work alone or with someone else, it is a good idea to record yourself and play it back.

To the teacher

Elements of Pronunciation combines the well-known pronunciation practice books – *Weak Forms, Clusters, Link-up, Contractions* and *Stress Time* – into one volume. The book is divided into five sections which correspond to the five original publications. Dialogues have been carefully selected so that the material can be used with students from intermediate level upwards, and, by selection, much of the material can be used at a lower level.

The recordings have been re-edited to make them easier to use. For each dialogue, the recording on the cassette now consists of:
1. A 'listen and repeat' section which picks out and drills the particular pronunciation point practised in the dialogue.
2. The dialogue is recorded straight through at natural speed.
3. A paused version of the dialogue with bleeps to indicate where students should repeat. The pauses usually occur at the end of each utterance, except where one speaker's part is exceptionally long and is therefore divided into smaller sections for repetition.

The recordings are slightly different for *Stress Time*. There is no initial 'listen and repeat' section, and the dialogues are recorded twice – the first time straight through with a tap in the background to indicate the stress, the second time with no tap but with pauses and bleeps to allow students to repeat. See the Introduction to the section on *Stress Time* for ways of using these dialogues.

Elements of Pronunciation can be used in class with a teacher, in a language laboratory with or without a teacher, or by a student working alone at home with the use of a cassette recorder.

Suggestions for use

Here is a suggested procedure which you may like to follow or adapt:
1. Before concentrating on the particular pronunciation point, use the dialogue for listening comprehension – it is important for students to get a sense of the meaning and pronunciation

of the whole. Students listen to the complete unpaused version of the dialogue and answer comprehension questions to ensure that they have understood the situation, the relationship between the speakers, what has just happened, what is likely to happen, etc. For many of the dialogues there will be no right answers as much is implied, so students should be encouraged to put forward and discuss various points of view.

2. Students practise the initial 'listen and repeat' section, using the recording. You may like to extend this and pick out other items yourself. It is useful to start with one phrase and slowly extend the repetition to the whole utterance, e.g. 'with Alan', 'going with Alan', 'are you going with Alan', 'are you going to the party with Alan' etc.

3. Students listen again to the complete unpaused version of the dialogue, this time concentrating on the pronunciation as well as on the meaning.

4. Students use the paused version of the dialogue for repetition. They work alone.

5. Students work in pairs, taking one part each and repeating the dialogue after the recording, using the paused version.

6. Students read the dialogue in pairs without the recording. Their version could be recorded so they can then listen to themselves. (You may want them to memorise and perform some of the shorter dialogues.)

7. You may now like to ask students some questions about the dialogue which encourage them to use the particular pronunciation point in their answers, e.g. Dialogue 114:
   Q. What do the speakers say will happen to all the lady's anxieties and problems?
   A. They'll disappear.

Weak Forms

Introduction

A good practical grasp of the weak forms of English is essential
to good pronunciation and listening comprehension. This section
contains dialogues in which some of the more important weak
forms are contextualised. The items selected are all weak forms
containing the 'neutral' vowel. The first group of dialogues
features individual weak forms. The remaining dialogues are
devoted to a selection of sequences of two or three of the items
that have first been treated individually. The pronunciation of
each weak form is indicated in phonetic transcription, in the
heading.

Featured items are identified in the text in a lighter type face.
There may, however, be words not in light type which need to be
pronounced weakly if the dialogue is to be spoken properly. Most
of such items are featured specifically elsewhere in the book, and
their incidental occurrence in other dialogues can be treated as
useful revision or as a foretaste. But primary attention should be
given to the weak forms actually specified in the heading.

*An asterisk after a word indicates that it should be pronounced in
its strong form.* It is not possible in such a short book to give
explanations of the circumstances in which weak and strong
forms are appropriate:

    e.g. *the* – /ðə/ only before consonant sounds.

        from – strong in final position.

        that – all demonstratives strong.

Phonetics handbooks will readily provide the relevant basic
information, and should be consulted.

1 a /ə/

A   So what went wrong?
B   Well, you said all I needed was a pencil, a ruler, a piece of wood,
    a saw, a hammer and a couple of nails.
A   I said you needed a pencil, a ruler, a piece of wood, a saw, a
    hammer, a couple of nails, and a bit of common *sense*.†
B   Ah.

   † Words in italics should be given extra emphasis.

2 an /ən/

A   I need an immediate answer.
B   You shall have an answer. In an hour or so.
A   I must have an answer now.
B   It's not an easy decision to make. But if you insist on an
    immediate answer, it must be an extremely reluctant 'no'.
A   Oh.
B   Sorry.
A   Well, I suppose if you *do* need an extra hour or so . . .
B   But I don't, now, do I? An extra drink, yes. Have one?
    Before you go?

5

3 the /ðə/†

A   **Now the* exercise – the drill.**
     LISTEN: **The pear, the peach, the pineapple.**
     The* apple, the* orange, the* apricot.
     REPEAT.

B   **The pear, the peach, the pineapple.**
     The* apple, the* orange, the* apricot.

A   **The father, the mother. The* uncle, the* aunt.**

B   **The father, the mother. The* uncle, the* aunt.**

A   REVISION: **Apple. Pear.**

B   **The* apple. The pear.**

A   **Good.** NEW WORD: **End.**

B   **The* end.**

A   **Good.**

B   **Good.**

† Only before consonant sounds.
* Indicates a strong form.

4 some /səm/

A   Mm! Delicious, John! Can I have some more?
    How d'you make it, by the way?
B   Oh, you need some lean meat, some vegetables, some butter,
    flour, salt. Chillies. Some garlic, if you've got some*. Lots of
    things.
A   Who gave you the recipe?
B   Oh, some* woman I know.
A   Well, it really *is* some* dish!
B   So is *she*! Now, you did say you wanted some more, darling?
A   Well . . . if I'm to have some pudding, perhaps not.

5 and /ən(d)/

A   A whisky and soda. A whisky and water. A brandy and soda.
    Three gin and tonics with ice and lemon, and two gin and
    tonics *without* ice and lemon. And another whisky and soda.
    And a glass of water for me.
B   A whisky and soda. A whisky and water. A brandy and soda.
    Three gin and tonics with ice and lemon, and two gin and
    tonics *without* ice and lemon. And another whisky and soda.
    And a glass of water for you, sir. Right, sir.
A   No, wait a minute. Let me change that. Let's have . . .

6 but /bət/

A But **I** can't. **I'm** sorry, but **I** can't.
B But **you must.**
A **I'd like to.** But **I** can't.
B But **I'm depending on you.** We're *all* **depending on you.**
A **I'll do** *anything* **but that.**
B But *no* **one else could do it as well as you!**
A **Why not ask Dalia? She could do it even** *better*.
B But **she's too** *busy*.

7 of /əv/

A **There you are, Betty – a bottle of milk. Three boxes of matches.
A can of beans. Two bags of sugar. A packet of biscuits. A jar of
jam. A bottle of lemon squash. And two tins of peaches.
That's the lot, I think. OK?**
B **Thanks, dear. How much was it? Ugh! What's this in the bottom
of the bag?**
A **Oh, yes. And half a dozen eggs.**

8 from /frəm/

A **I had a call** from **Bill.**
B From **Bill? Who's Bill?**
A **He's very special. He telephones me** from **overseas. Every day.**
B **Where from*?**
A **Oh** – from **wherever he happens to be: Africa, America, Asia . . .
From Australia, this time.**
B **He** *must* **be special.**
A **He hates to be away** from **me.**
B **Of course, George sometimes rings** *me* from **the factory.
The trouble is,** *he* **always reverses the** *charges*!
A **Oh,** *Bill* **reverses the charges, of course.**

9 at /ət/

A   **Where were you** at **one o'clock?**
B   At **one o'clock?** At **my mother's.**
A   At **two o'clock?**
B   At **my sister's.**
A   **And** at **one thirty?**
B   At **one thirty, Officer?** At **a point approximately half way**
     between my mother's and my sister's.
A   At **Sam's Bar, in fact?**
B   **Only for five minutes,** at **the most. Why?**

10 them /ðəm/

A I saw them **together.**
B *Where* **did you see** them?
A **In the town.**
B *When* **did you see** them?
A **This morning.**
B **Did you** *say* **anything to** them?
A **I told** them **I should tell you.**
B **Which you've now done. Thank you.**
A **Aren't you going to send for** them?
B **No need. I've already invited** them **for dinner.**
A *Them**? **Both of** them? **Together?**
B **Like to join us?**

11 us /əs/

A **Let's ask him to let** us **go.**
B **He won't let** us **go.**
A **He can't keep** us **forever.**
B **Course he can.**
A **Let's escape.**
B **He'd catch** us. **Anyway, I like it here. He treats** us **well. Gives** us **lovely clothes. Lovely food – everything.**
A **He must give** us **our** *freedom*!
B **Don't be greedy.**

12 that /ðət/

A **We all know** that **we face problems. We know** that **we face difficulties. We are all aware** that **the difficulties** that **we face are not difficulties** that **will be overcome immediately, or** that **will be overcome easily. We all recognise** that **the problems** that **confront us are not problems** that **will be solved overnight. But I sometimes wonder if we realise . . . if we realise** *sufficiently* that . . .
B **That** *that** **was the clock striking** *two*, **Frank! Go to sleep!**
A **Sorry, dear. Didn't know it was so late. My big day, tomorrow, you know. Ah, well. Goodnight.**
B **It's a lovely speech, Frank.**

13 as /əz/

A   As **John couldn't come, he asked me to come** as **a substitute.
But** *you're* **not** *Julie*.

B   **No.** As **Julie couldn't come, she sent me –** as **a substitute.**

A   **You know, it looks to me** as **if John and Julie . . .**

B   **It does, doesn't it?**

A   **I disapprove of such tricks,** as **a rule.**

B   **So do I.** As **a rule.**

A   **However, . . .**

B   **Well?**

14   as . . . as /əz . . . əz/

A   **You're** as **cunning** as **a fox.**

B   **Cunning? I'm** as **innocent** as **a child!**

A   **And** as **slippery** as **a snake!**

B   **Anyway, believe me, this necklace is unique! And old! Old** as **the hills!**

A   **And gold?**

B   As *good* **as.***

> * Probably strong in this final position, but in very familiar speech *could* be weak.

15 than /ðən/

A **Carol's more sensible** than **Jenny, prettier** than **Jenny,**
   cleverer than **Jenny, and richer** than **Jenny.** So why do I like
   Jenny more than **Carol?**
B **And why does Jenny like** *me* **more than you?**

16 there /ðə(r)/

A There **ought to be someone here.**
B There **ought to be.** But there **isn't, I don't think.**
A There's **a light in that room.**
B **Let's take a look.**
A **Oh, my God!**
B **Mm. It looks as if** there's **someone here after all, poor chap.**
   There's **a phone over there*. Better ring the police.**

17 am /əm/†

A **Why** am **I leaving? Where** am **I going? Who** am **I going with?**
   Where am **I staying? When** am **I coming back?** *Am** **I coming**
   back? These are questions you'll probably wish to ask me,
   Barbara, but . . .
B **Now, darling. How** am **I looking?**

   † 'I'm' – see Dialogue 104.

18 are /ə(r)/†

A **These** are **the best.**
B **These** are **nice, too.**
A **Mm. But these** are **more suitable, don't you think?**
B **They're a bit old-fashioned, perhaps.**
A **And they're a bit flashy, I suppose.**
B **They** are*, **yes. Anyway,** there are **no more in the shop. And we**
   must **give them their present today.**
A **So what** are **we going to do?**
B **Well, Freddie and Paulette** are *both* **a bit old-fashioned, you know.**
A **Yes. But in a flashy sort of way.**

   † 'You're', 'we're' etc. – see Dialogues 108 and 109.

19 was /wəz/

A The man was *kind*.
B He was **generous**.
A He *was**. Extremely generous.
B He was **popular**.
A Oh, he was **very very popular**.
B So when we heard he was . . .
A Yes.
B I was . . .
A We *all* were.

20 has /əz/ †

A The bus has **gone already, Janet**.
B **Which** has **gone? The Sixty?**
A The Sixty Six has **gone as well**.
B **It must have gone early, unless my watch** has **stopped. Look –
   Madge** has **missed it too. And Rose** has **missed it. No use
   running, Rose!**
A **Gosh –** *Rose* has **put on a pound or two since she last ran for a
   bus! Oops! No use running, Rose! It's gone!**

† 'He's', 'Jack's', etc. – see Dialogue 105.

21 have /əv/ †

A The wheels **have dropped off**! The wings have **broken**! It's **useless**!
B How many times have **you flown it**?
A Only once! I wouldn't have **bought it** if I'd **known**!
B And I suppose if *they* **hadn't known**, they wouldn't have **reduced it to half price**. Anyway, we all have* to **learn**, eh? Oh, by the way, I've **bought you this**. Got it from Walker's. Like it?
A Oh, it's **marvellous, Dad**. Thanks. They had one in Gray's **sale**, but I couldn't **afford it**. Thanks, Dad.

† 'I've', 'you've', etc. – see Dialogues 116 and 117.

22 had /əd/ †

A All our **money** had **gone**.
B My **jewels** had **gone**.
A Our **clothes** had **gone**.
B The **passports** had **gone**.
A The air **tickets** had **gone**.
B **Everything** had **been taken**.
A **Everything we had***. It'd all **gone**.
B Except the present we'd **bought you**.
A They **hadn't taken that, fortunately**.
B Hope you **like it**.

† 'We'd', 'you'd', etc. – see Dialogues 122, 123 and 124.

23 does /dəz/

A He *does** sound nice. But I hope you won't mind if I ask him a
few questions, Millicent, such as where does he . . .

B Where does he live? What sort of family does he come from?
Who . . . *Whom* does he know that *we* know? What does he do
for a living? How much money does he make? That sort of
thing, you mean, mother?

A Yes, dear. And also what does . . .

B What does he see in *me*?

A Apart from your money, dear, yes.

24 can /kən/

A She can **play the flute.**
She can **paint pictures.**
She can **write poems.**
She can **grow plants.**
She can do *most* things.
What can *I* do? I can't do *any* of the things *she* can*!

B You can **fight.**

A Yes, but who want a girl who can fight?

B *I* do.

25 must /məs(t)/

A   **Tell me what I must do.**

B   **You** must **go to them. And you** must **confess. Tell them it was**
you.

A   **I suppose I must*.**

B   **You** must *trust* **them. They'll be lenient‡, I'm sure.**

A   **Yes. Yes, I suppose I** must **tell them** *everything*.

B   **Well, perhaps not** *quite* **everything.**

A   **Oh?**

B   **No need to mention** *me*, **for instance.**

‡ lenient: not severe, tolerant

Selected combinations of two weak forms†

26 /əv + ə, ən, ðə, əs, ðəm/

A You hate all of them.
B No. But I dislike *one* of them. Roger, I think his name is.
A Because of the way he dresses, I suppose.
B No. Because of a *word* he used in front of an old lady.
A Oh, yes. I heard. But she's so old-*fashioned*!
B Some* of us *are*, I suppose. And anyway, it's hardly a *new* word, is it?

27 /tə + ðə, ðəm/

A All those friends of yours overseas – why not write to them? Or *go* somewhere. Go to the cinema. Or to the beach. Or to the tennis club. You *can't* sit brooding‡ about that girl all the time.
B Yes, I think I *will* write to them.
A Good.
B She usually goes to the Post Office about five.

‡ brood: to think about (troubles etc.) for a long time

28 /ət + ə, ən, ðə, ðəm/

A 'Stop *screeching*', did you say? Don't you know I once sang at a concert? At an inter*national* concert? At the biggest theatre in town? You must look at my press cuttings!
B I *will* look at them, darling. But I have to be at a meeting at a quarter past seven. And I *would* like a bath. Do hurry up. Please!

† Where *single* weak forms from the selected *pairs* occur, these are also identified in the text.

29 /fə(r) + ə, ðə, səm/

A How long have I come for*? For a **month**. Why **have I come**?
Oh . . . for some **sunshine**. For the **sea**. For some **good food**.
For the **wine**. For a **bit of excitement**, I suppose. **Why did** *you*
come?
B For the **money**. I **work here**.
A Not *all* the time, I hope.

30 /frəm + ə, ən, ðə, səm, ðəm/

A I got it from an **old friend, who** got it from a **friend, who got it**
from some **friends, who borrowed it** from the **Browns**. Where
did you get the idea it was *stolen* from them?
B I got it from a **friend. A mutual friend**.

31 /ə(r) + ə, ən, ðə, səm/

A These are a **new type**. And those are the **type you had before**. Oh – **here** are some **more**. These are the **very latest**. And the **best**. **Just arrived**.

B **Yes**, I can see those are an **entirely different model**. **Where** are the **handles, by the way**?

A Oh, er . . . **Modern design**, you see. **No handles**. **No handles** *needed*, you see.

B Mm. Ah! **What** are the *plastic* **things in the bottom of the box**?

A **Plas** . . . Oh, yes. **Optional extras**, you see.

32 /wəz + ə, ən, ðə, səm/

A *That* was a **poor meal**.

B It was an *extremely* **poor meal**.

A The **soup** was a **disgrace**.

B The **meat** was the **toughest ever**.

A **All we got for pudding** was some **tinned fruit**.

B **Where** was the **special sauce**?

A **Where** was the **special dessert**?

B **Nothing** was the **same as last year**.

A **Except the bill**.

B And *that* was a **bit bigger, actually**.

33 /wə(r) + ə, ən, ðə/

A **You** were a **star**. **You** were the **greatest actress of your generation**. **You** were the **most beautiful woman of your time**. **You** were an **inspiration to us all**.

B And *you* were an **incorrigible liar, Rupert**.

A **Beatrice**!

B **You still** *are*, **thank God**.

34 /ðə(r)+ə(r), wə(r)

A There were **five.**
B There were **four.**
A There were **five. At** *least* **five.**
B There were **only four.**
A **Well, anyway,** *one* **thing's certain.**
B **What?**
A There are **only four now.**
B There are **only** *three*, **in fact.**

Selected combinations of three weak forms†

35 /ən(d), bət + əv + ə, ən, ðə, səm/

A **The Company Chairman reminded everybody** of the **problems
we face.**

B And of the **difficulties before us.**

A And of the **hard road that lies ahead.**

B And of an **ever increasing need to make sacrifices.**

A And of a **need to increase our efforts.**

B **He spoke not only** of the **problems.**

A But of the **new opportunities.**

B And of the **new challenges.**

A And of some **recent plans.**

B And of a **bright future.**

A And of a **bright, though distant future.**

† Where *pairs* from the selected *threes* occur, these are also identified in the text.

36 /ən(d), bət + ət + ə, ðə/

A George **wasn't** at the **meeting,** but at a **party.** A *wild* one.

B **Not** at the **meeting?** And at a **wild party? How disgraceful!
Where?**

A **In town.** And at the **house of a friend of yours** – Josephine. You
really must speak to George.

B I shall *certainly* **do that.** But at the **moment,** *she's* the one I must
speak to! At Josephine's you say? And at a **wild party** *I* wasn't
invited to?

37 /ən(d), bət + fə(r) + ə, ðə, səm/

A I know why you came – **you came** for a **drink,** and for some **food,**
and for a **talk with the boys,** and for the **television.**

B I *swear* I **came here not** for a **drink** and for the **various other
things you mention,** but for the **chance to see your pretty,
smiling face again!**

A **Oh, Victor!**

B **So bring the food and drink, and switch on the television, and tell
me where the boys are, my darling** – **there's a good girl.**

38 /ər + ət + ə, ðə/

A My **parents** are at a **meeting and** my **sisters** are at the **cinema.**
   I'm all alone. Like to join me?
B **Sorry, but** *my* **parents** are at the **theatre, and my little sisters** are
   at the **moment expecting me to bath them and put them to bed.**
A **Oh.**
B **Like to read them a story?**

39 /wəz + ət + ə, ən, ðə/

A **Last year it** was at a **restaurant. The year before, it** was at an
   expensive hotel, and the year before that, it was at the **factory**
   itself – in the canteen. And that was the *best* **party, I thought.**
B **Yes. But** *that* was at the **time when your** *wife* was in **charge of**
   the canteen!

40 /wər + ət + ə, ðə/

A **How terrible! Just imagine,** *we* were at a **concert, enjoying**
   ourselves, while *you*, **poor thing,** were at the **hospital, with a**
   broken leg!
B **And a couple of very nice nurses!**

41 /ə+frəm+ə, ðə/

A   Steven and Mark are from the **Ministry. Robert and Sam** are
from the **Local Government Offices. And the others** are from a
variety of interested organisations. We're here to discuss
co-ordination. Who are you?
B   **Simon and I** are from the **Ministry. The other members of our**
committee are coming soon. We're here to discuss *co-operation*.
And this is *our* room.

42 /wəz+frəm+ə, ðə/

A   *This* was from the **garden!** *That* was from the **garden! And** *this*
was from the **garden! Our own garden! Aren't they superb?**
B   **And look at this! The best of all! This** was from the **garden, too,**
was it?
A   **That** was from a **shop.**
B   **No, no, no. I meant** *that*. *That's* **the one I meant – not** *that*.
A   **Good.**

43   /əv + əs, ðəm + ə(r), wə(r), kən, məst/

A   Only three of us are **on the short-list, and** *he's* **the favourite.**

B   Surely *none* of them **can know about his private life? Or they wouldn't** *consider* **promoting him! One** of us must **do our duty!**

A   **If all** of us were **perfect, Martin, I'd agree with you. But I** *must** con*fess* . . .

B   **Yes, James? Needless to say, you can trust** *me*! **Absolutely!**

A   **I'm glad to hear it. But perhaps more important, in this case:** *You* **can trust** *me* – **I'm sorry to say.**

44   /ðə(r) + ə, wə, wəz + ə, ən, səm/

A   **Anything for me?**

B   There were some **telephone calls. I said you'd ring back.** There are some **letters.** Oh, yes – and there was an **inquiry. Someone asking about something called Weak Forms. Have we got any?**

Clusters

Introduction

This section aims to help students who can pronounce individual
English consonants, as in *s*at, *c*at or *r*at, but experience difficulty
when these occur in clusters, as in *scr*eam, and even greater
difficulty when words containing clusters occur in connected
speech. It consists of dialogues in which most of the clusters
encountered in English are featured in context. Each dialogue
concentrates on a specified cluster or group of clusters, indicated
in phonemic transcription in the headings and in italics in the
text. There are four parts:
- Two consonant clusters in word initial position, e.g. *sp*eak.
- Three consonant clusters in word initial position, e.g. *str*ong.
- Two consonant clusters in word final position, e.g. loo*ks*.
- Three consonant clusters in word final position, e.g. ga*sps*.

Part One: CCV

45 pl bl pr br

A   *Pl*ease go, *Br*ian.
B   I *br*ing you a beautiful *pr*esent, and you tell me to **go**!
A   *Br*ian, I ap*pr*eciate the *pr*esent, but...
B   Would you *pr*efer a ***bl*ack** † one?
A   *Br*own suits me perfectly, but...
B   Or a *bl*ue one?
A   But if your ***br*other** finds you here...
B   My *br*other? But surely *Br*ett's gone to...
A   *Pr*obably that's him now.
B   *Bl*ast! *Bl*ast!
A   Oh. Perhaps it's only the *br*ead man.
B   Good.
A   No. No, it **is** *Br*ett. *Br*ett, darling...
B   *Br*ett, you *pr*obably won't **believe** this, but, er...

   † Words in bold type should be given extra emphasis.

46 tr dr tw

A How are you *tr*avelling, *Tr*evor?
B By *tr*ain. The *tw*elve *tw*enty.
A Shall I *dr*ive you to the station?
B In all this *dr*eadful *tr*affic? Oh, no – I'll *tr*y to get a taxi.
A It's no *tr*ouble. Of course, if you don't *tr*ust my *dr*iving...
B Oh, I *tr*ust your ***dr*iving**, all right.
A Fine. *Tw*elve at your flat, then?
B Thanks. But *Tr*icia, the *tr*ip really is ***tr*emendously** important and...
A Mm?
B Well, the *tr*ain really **does** leave at *tw*elve *tw*enty.

47 kl gl kr gr kw

A You're back *qu*ickly. Didn't you go to the *cr*icket *cl*ub?
B Yes, I went.
A Was it *cr*owded?
B *Qu*ite *cr*owded.
A Was *Gr*eg there?
B *Gr*eg was there, yes. And *Qu*entin.
A But surely *Qu*entin **hates** *cr*icket.
B That's why they had a slight disagreement today.
A They *qu*arrelled?
B *Gr*eg threw a *gl*ass of beer at *Qu*entin.
A Oh dear.
B He missed, however.
A Mm. Shall I take your *cl*othes to the *cl*eaners?

48 fl fr

A   *Fl*atter me, *Fr*ed.
B   *Fl*atter you, *Fl*orrie?
A   *Fr*ank *fl*atters me, *Fr*ed.
B   *Fr*ank *fl*atters everybody.
A   He says I create a *fl*ame in his heart!
B   A *fl*ame in his heart?
A   A furious *fl*ame! He says I drive him **fr**antic!
B   You drive me *fr*antic too, *Fl*orrie.
A   Oh, *Fr*ed! You old *fl*atterer!
B   *Fr*y the fish, *Fl*orrie.

49 θr

A   Only *thr*eepence?
B   Only *thr*eepence a *thr*ill.
A   I'll have *thr*ee, please.

50 sp st sk

A   Ladies and gentlemen...

B   *Sp*eak up, *St*anley!

A   I *st*and before you...

B   *Sp*eak up, *St*anley!

A   On this *Sch*ool *Sp*eech Day...

B   Do *sp*eak **up**!

A   ON THIS *SCH*OOL *SP*EECH DAY...

B   *St*op **shouting**, *St*anley!

A   And I *sp*eak for both my wife and myself, when I say...

B   *Sp*eak up, *St*anley!

A   *SP*EAK UP *ST*ANLEY!!

51 sm sn sl sw

A Is *Sn*owy at home? *Sn*owy *Sm*ith?
B He's *sl*eeping. Go away.
A *Sl*eeping? Where?
B In there. Why do you *sm*ile?
A Perhaps *Sn*owy is in there. But he isn't asleep.
B I swear he's *sl*eeping.
A When *Sn*owy sleeps, *Sn*owy *sn*ores. And when he *sn*ores, he **sn**ores! Hey, *Sn*owy! *Sn*owy! *Sn*owy, it's *Sl*im!
B You see – no *sn*oring, *Sl*im.
A It's the first time. Hey, *Sn*owy!
B Doesn't he look *sw*eet?
A *Sn*owy! Wake up! Wake up, *Sn*owy! *SN*OWY!
B And now there's one *sl*ight *sn*ag‡.
A A *sn*ag?
B The *sm*all problem of what to do with **you**, *Sl*im.

‡ snag: unexpected difficulty

52 ʃr

A I shall *shr*iek!
B *Shr*iek?
A *Shr*iek!
B Why *shr*iek?
A *Shr*iek with terror!
B They're only *shr*imps. A *shr*imp isn't anything to *shr*iek about. If there were a **shark**, of course...
A Oh!!
B Ah, well, *shr*impies – back into the water.
A Good.
B What **else** is there for tea?

Part Two: CCCV

53   spl spr

A   What a *spl*endid *Spr*ing day!
B   A ***spl*endid** day!
A   We'll *spr*ead our towels!
B   *Spl*endid!
A   We'll *spr*awl in the sun!
B   *Spr*awl in the sun! *Spl*endid!
A   We'll *spr*int along the beach!
B   We'll ***spr*int**?
A   **I'll** *spr*int.
B   *Spl*endid!

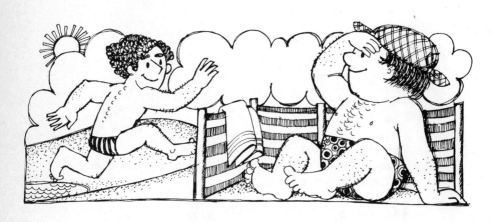

54   str

A   How *str*ong you are, Mr *Str*ong!
B   All the *Str*ongs are *str*ong.
A   But you're the *str*ongest!
B   How *str*ange you are, Miss *Str*ange! I suppose all the *Str*anges are *str*ange.
A   Yes?
B   Ouch!
A   And *str*ong!

55 skr skw

A If you like noises
B Noises in the night
A *Squ*eaks, for example
B *Squ*eals, for example
A *Scr*atching and *scr*aping
B *Squ*elching and *squa*wking
A Then this is the place for you
B And if you like *scr*eeches
A *Scr*eeches and *scr*eams
B Oh, if you like **screams**
A You'll love it here
B **Do** you like noises?

Part Three: VCC

56 pt bd ps bz

A We were ro*bbed*!
B Stri*pped* of everything!
A They jum*ped* out into the road...
B And when we sto*pped*...
A They gra*bbed* me and thum*ped* me in the ri*bs*...
B And said if we didn't 'shut our tra*ps*‡'...
A We'd be sta*bbed*.
B They tied us with ro*pes*...
A And dum*ped* us in the back of a van.
B Finally they dro*pped* us at the bottom of these ste*ps*...
A And the **polite** one I descri*bed* to you...
B Oh, yes – **he** said he was sorry we'd been 'distur*bed*'!
A And ho*ped* the ro*pes* weren't too tight!
B Actually **he** was rather charming!

‡ traps: mouths (slang)

57 ts dz

A He just si*ts*.
B That's all he does.
A All day – si*ts* and si*ts*.
B Occasionally he rea*ds*.
A And ea*ts*.
B But he ea*ts* very little.
A We tell him he nee*ds* fresh air.
B He nee*ds* frien*ds*.
A He used to have lo*ts* of frien*ds*.
B Loa*ds* of frien*ds*.
A But now he just si*ts* and broo*ds*.
B And he won't even **speak** to his ki*ds*.
A He **still** says he has no regre*ts*, of course.
B No regre*ts*. Mm.
A Ah, well. What's the film at the Ri*tz*?

58 tʃt dʒd

A We mar*ched* all day.
B We pi*tched* our ten*ts* by the river.
A Some of us sle*pt*. Some wa*tched*.
B In the morning, we bri*dged* the river.
A And mar*ched* again until we rea*ched* the battlefield.
B The battle ra*ged* for two nights.
A Some of us do*dged* the shells.
B Some of us mana*ged* to survive.
A The privile*ged* ones?

59 nt nd

A He we*nt*. And he never retur*ned*.
B He we*nt* when?
A Oh, about the e*nd* of September.
B Well, I war*ned* you.
A Don't remi*nd* me.
B You ca*n't* say you were*n't* war*ned*.
A Anyway, he se*nt* the re*nt*.
B Have you fou*nd* a new tena*nt*?
A Yes – a frie*nd*. Peg Bo*nd*. There wo*n't* be any problems.
B I hope there wo*n't*.
A You do*n't* know Peg, of course?
B Well...I once le*nt* her a pou*nd*!

60 nθ ns nz

A Bye, Flore*nce*. See you in a mo*nth*. Oh – if Vi*nce* pho*nes*...
B Vi*nce* who?
A Vi*nce* Bur*ns*.
B Vi*nce* Bur*ns*? Not **the** Vi*nce* Bur*ns*?
A Yes. If he pho*nes*, tell him...
B You know Vi*nce* Bur*ns*?
A Course. And if he pho*nes*...
B I have a cha*nce* to talk to Vi*nce* Bur*ns*?
A Say I'll be back on the te*nth*, probably...
B 'She'll be back on the te*nth*, Mr Bur*ns*...'
A And if I'm not...
B 'And if she's not, Mr Bur*ns*, my name is Flore*nce*...'

61 ntʃ ndʒ

A Tomorrow we lau*nch* our new sales campaign. I'm giving a lu*nch* at our city bra*nch*. In the staff lou*nge*. Do come.
B D'you know, Bla*nche*, your last lu*nch* added an i*nch* to my waistline.
A I see no cha*nge*.
B Look. I have a pau*nch*! I'm going on a diet!
A Oh.
B Immediately after your lu*nch*.

62 ft vd fθ fs vz

A He's not on the fourth floor now, he's been mo*ved* – to the fi*fth*. Use the li*ft*. I'll ring to say you've arri*ved*.
B No hurry. Er...how is he, Nurse?
A I think he's impro*ved*. Still cou*ghs* a lot, of course.
B And he beha*ves* all right, does he?
A Oh, yes. We have plenty of lau*ghs*! We'll miss him when he lea*ves*!
B He lo*ves* pretty nurses, Grandad does! It's a family weakness! By the way, he wanted me to bring him this gi*ft*. For his special favourite – a nurse called So*ft*.
A How lovely!
B Funny name, So*ft*, isn't it?
A Yes. But I've got u*sed* to it.
B Oh. Sorry.
A Well, I'll ring to say you've arri*ved*.
B I'm **sorry**!

63 θt ðd θs ðz

A Who ba*ths* you?
B **She** ba*ths* me. She's **always** ba*thed* me.
A Who clo*thes* you?
B **She** clo*thes* me. She's **always** clo*thed* me.
A And yet she loa*thes* you?
B She's **always** loa*thed* me!

64 sp st sk zd

A

1st JUNE

Ocean Hotel. First class breakfast.
   Toast beautifully crisp.
Went for a brisk walk.
Lazed by the pool.
Splendid lunch. Roast chicken.
   Braised celery.
Gazed at the sea. Dozed happily
   till dusk.
Dressed for dinner.
At dinner, met a most **charming**
   woman!

B

1st JUNE

Ocean Hotel. Breakfast – the worst
   ever!
Was stung by a wasp.
Got lost.
Having got lost,
   missed lunch.
Also,
   missed the last post.
Tore my best dress. Late for dinner.
At dinner, met a most **dreary**
   man!

Part Four: VCCC

65 kts ksθ kst

A He's one of our most important conta*cts*. But difficult. How did you do it, Samantha?

B Oh, he mi*xed* me a drink. We rela*xed*. And I coa*xed* him into agreeing to look at our produ*cts*. I've fi*xed* an appointment for the si*xth*. And if he rea*cts* favourably . . .

A Excellent.

B He's sweet, by the way – as I've always said.

A Hm! That confli*cts* with **John's** view of him!

B Well, John **always** contradi*cts* my opinions.

A And, of course, you differ in certain **other** important respe*cts*!

66 mpt mps mft mfs

A His pro*mpt* action ultimately led to their arrest. Good triu*mphs* over evil in the end, you know, Mrs Smith – as I've always said.
B Mm. Of course, he got those **lu*mps*** on his head when they ju*mped* on him and du*mped* him down that well. And he still li*mps*.
A Yes, yes.
B Anyway, I'm glad to know that good triu*mphed* in the end.
A Indeed.
B What punishment will they get, by the way?

67 nθs nst

A If only they could've waited! Even six mo*nths*!
B Or a couple of mo*nths*, anyway.
A We've nothing **agai*nst*** him, of course.
B Nothing at all.
A They're so young and inexperie*nced*!
B Yes. But how experie*nced* were we?
A We courted for **years** before our engagement was annou*nced*!
B Years, dear?
A Well, if you're sure they'll be happy...
B I'm convi*nced*.

68 ntʃt ndʒd

A 'He lu*nged* ‡ at me with a knife. I pu*nched* him. He dropped it. He cri*nged* ‡ in the corner, teeth tightly cle*nched*, eyes filled with hatred. "I'll be reve*nged*!" he snarled. I pu*nched* him again. Harder...'
B ...Then I lu*nched* with Jenny, as arra*nged*.
A Oh, hello!
B Nearly finished your chapter?

‡ lunge: make a sudden forward movement
‡ cringe: move back or down in fear

69 ŋkt ŋks

A   You see, as the exchange rate si*nks*, the value of your savings shri*nks*. But if you **ba*nked*** your money, instead of keeping it . . . wherever you keep it . . . it could earn **interest**, to some extent li*nked* to the cost of living.

B   No, tha*nks*.

A   Where **do** you keep it, by the way?

70   lpt lkt lps lts lks

A   She su*lks*.

B   She always **has** su*lked*.

A   And you should hear the insu*lts*!

B   She insu*lts* him all the time.

A   She never he*lps* him.

B   Never **has** he*lped*.

A   Well, we warned him.

B   Oh, we warned him.

A   We forecast the resu*lts*.

B   We did.

A   Finish your ice-cream, Harold – before it me*lts*.

71 lmd lmz

A   One of your most famous fi*lms* was about an enormous monster
     that overwhe*lms* a city. You played the monster, didn't you?
B   That's right. It was fi*lmed* in the studio, of course. And the city
     I overwhe*lmed* was only a small, plaster-board model. Even so,
     I managed to break my **toe** in rehearsal!
A   I'll never forget the bit where you kicked the Marine Hotel
     into the sea!
B   With my **left** foot, you'd notice!

72 Iθs Ist

A   I was alone. Missing you.
B   So whi*lst* I was away, you opened my **last** bottle of champagne!
A   I drank your health, darling!
B   From **two** glasses?
A   And **my** health, darling! I drank **both** our hea*lths*!

73 sps sts spt skt sks

A   The hotel caters mainly for touri*sts*.
B   As usual, they ga*sped* in terror as we whi*sked* away ‡ the bedclothes.
A   And as we whi*sked* away the pillows, there were more ga*sps*...
B   Even though these ta*sks* were performed nicely.
A   None of the gue*sts* ever reque*sts* a second night in the haunted room.
B   As ho*sts*...
A   Resident gho*sts*...
B   We find this so disappointing.

‡ whisk away: take quickly and suddenly

74 fts fθs

A   We have now completed our customer survey, Sir. Of the total numbers going up to the Arts and Cra*fts*, and Gi*fts* Departments, **three** fi*fths* used the escalator, **two** fi*fths* used the li*fts*, and **one** fifth used the steps, Sir.

B   **Six** fi*fths*, Mr To*fts*?

75 Conclusion

A Now you've *practised* lo*ts* of *cl*usters.
B Yes, but only with two and *three* consona*nts*.
B All right, then – say 'Four *twelfths* make two si*xths*.'
B Easy. Four twe*l*...

Link-up

Introduction

This section consists of dialogues designed to encourage students to link words together smoothly and naturally, in connected speech, in the way that native speakers normally do. It aims to help especially those learners who tend to pronounce each word as though it were isolated, or to make excessive use of the glottal stop before words beginning with vowels.

Intensive, contextualised practice is provided in linking:
1. Words ending in a *consonant* sound to words beginning with a *vowel* sound:

    e.g.   read it   brush up   sing it

2. Words ending in a *vowel* sound to words beginning with a *vowel* sound:

    e.g.   you are   I ought   after all

Each dialogue features a particular link or combination of links, the basis of organisation and selection being place and manner of articulation. So, for example, Dialogue 76 is devoted to linking p and b to words beginning with a vowel; Dialogue 88 focusses on t, d, n and l, which have first been practised individually in separate dialogues.

Words printed in *italics* should be given extra emphasis.

Linking final consonant sounds to initial vowel sounds

One practice technique which many students find helpful is to treat the final consonant sound of a word as though it were transferred to the next word:

    e.g. Practise   put it off
         as though it were   pu-ti-toff

Used with care, this device helps to promote good linking. It should be noted, however, that though *linked* to words beginning with vowel sounds, final consonant sounds are not usually in fact fully *transferred* in English. Thus, for example, in the phrase 'stop anywhere', the p at the end of 'stop' is not strongly aspirated as it would be if 'any' became 'penny'. Though linked, 'stop' and 'anywhere' retain their identity.

Linking 'r'

When a word ending with a letter 'r' precedes a word beginning with a vowel sound, the 'r' is usually pronounced, and this linkage is indicated in the text:

> e.g.   after‿all

Linking final vowel sounds to initial vowel sounds

To help students to link vowel sounds to vowel sounds, a small w or j is included with the linker:

> e.g.   do‿it   he‿ate some
>   w   j

Here again, used judiciously, this device will help to promote natural linking. Care should be taken, however, not to exaggerate the link to a full, strong w or j, resulting in

> do-wit   he-yet

76 p b

A Now, the psychological test. Ready? Quickly say the first verb each *noun* brings to your mind. Don't stop and think. Is that clear? Don't stop and think.

B I hope it's clear, yes.

A Right. The first noun . . . 'Handbag.'

B Grab. Grab a handbag.

A 'Bank.'

B Rob a bank.

A 'Man.'

B Stab a man.

A Stab a man. Mm . . . er . . .

B Don't stop and think, Doctor! Don't stop and think!

77 t d

A I'm called 'Pat', and I don't like my name.
It isn't attractive.

B But 'Pat' isn't as bad as some names. What about 'Dot'?
Dot isn't attractive.

A Oh, no. Dot isn't at *all* nice, no . . . Even
Pat isn't as bad as *Dot* . . . What are *you* called, by the way?

B You've guessed it!

78 k g

A   I'd like a walk – I think I'll take the dog out, Betty.

B   I'd like a drink – I think I'll go to the 'Duke of York' and drink a cool lager.

A   *You'd* like a drink, Betty? *You'd* like a drink? Oh, well . . .
Let's *both* take the dog out, then!

B   Fine.

A   No, dammit. Let's leave the dog at *home*!

79 tʃ dʒ

A   George, it's not possible! Your *leg*! You *can't* judge a beauty contest today.

B   You know where my crutch is, Bertha.

A   Of course, dear. But George, I really think you should . . .

B   Fetch it!

80 f v

A   I give all my parties from five until seven . . .
    Arrive at five exactly, please.
B   Arrive at five – of course, Sir.
A   Leave at seven, punctually.
B   Leave at seven, Sir. Yes, Sir.
A   Then move off and have a really good time. Right?
B   Sir?
A   Well, my parties *do* have a . . . reputation, don't they?
    Mm?

81 θ ð

A   Are you going to the party with Alan?
B   I can't go with Alan.
A   Or with Eric?
B   I can't go with Eric.
A   Oh.
B   Why don't *you* go with *both* of them?
A   To tell you the truth, I can't go with *either*.
B   You're not going?
A   I'm going with Alec.
B   With Alec? Both of us?

82 s z

A   Is the boss in?
B   The boss is *out*.
A   The boss is *always* out.
B   He's expected soon. He's at lunch.
A   It's almost *four*!
B   He's always in time for tea.

83 ʃ

A   Your whisky, Sir. With the usual splash of soda.

B   Thank you. Now which dish is good today?

A   The fish is good.

B   Fresh, I hope?

A   Fresh, of course, Sir.

B   And to finish off . . .

A   The usual, Sir?

B   But with lemon squash, I think. Not soda.

84 m

A   Come into *this* room – it's warm in here.

B   Thank you.

A   You've come about Jim, I suppose.

B   Jim isn't doing well.

A   I'm afraid that's true.

B   Jim oughtn't to be bottom of the class.

A   But next term I think we'll see him improving.   I'm optimistic.

B   Last time I came I remember you said . . .

A   'I'm optimistic', yes. But this time I'm *especially* so. Now . . .
    Tea? Jam? Plum or strawberry?

85 ŋ

A   Did you win anything?

B   I won an apple. Did *you* win anything?

A   I won an orange.

B   John won an air ticket.

A   An air ticket to where?

B   To London, I think. But he doesn't think he can afford the time to go. He hopes he can exchange the prize for something different.

A   An orange, perhaps?

86 ŋ

A   Bring a ring and that lovely string of pearls.

B   Any particular ring, Edwina?

A   Bring a diamond ring, Alfred. Something a bit special.

B   Yes. They'll be putting *everything* in the window today.

A   Are you taking anything along, Alfred?

B   Something appropriate, my love.

A   Nothing *obtrusive*, Alfred?

B   I'm taking a brick, dear.

87 |

A   Next we'll interview Miss Val Underhill, I think.

B   Underhill? . . . Val Underhill? Erm . . . Did she fill in the form?

A   She did fill in the form.

B   Mm. Well it seems we didn't file it, then.

A   Well, if we've lost the form we'll obviously have to . . .

B   Sh!

A   Ah, good morning. Miss Underhill, I presume?
     Now, naturally we have your full application here . . .

B   All appropriate personal and professional information . . .

A   Nevertheless, we'd be grateful if you'd tell us . . .

B   It would be *useful* if you'd tell us something . . .

A   All about yourself, please.

88 t d n l

A What in the hell is *that*, Enid Evans?

B I bought it in a sale, Eddie.

A Well, it isn't *ideal*, to say the least, Enid.

B It isn't ideal, Eddie, no.

A In fact, I'd incline to call it . . .

B Well *don't* Eddie. Not unless you want your meal elsewhere.

A Sorry.

B Thank you.

A Enid, in fact now that I've looked at it *again*, I . . .

B Isn't it *awful*, Eddie?

89 t d n l s z

A Can I ride it, please, uncle?

B Yes, of course, if you ride it carefully.

A Can I go fast on it?

B Yes, if you go carefully.

A I can't ride it outside, I suppose, uncle?

B Perhaps it might be best if you practised in the garden a bit first.

A Then can I ride it in the road?

B Well, I'll see. Perhaps your dad wouldn't agree.

A But I know dad *would* agree. Definitely.

B Well, I'll ask.

A Don't ask.

90 tʃ dʒ ʃ s z

A When will you finish it?

B Finish it? Finish it? It's finished!

A Wallace, as I always admit . . .

B Yes?

A I'm no judge of sculpture.

B No.

A No judge of such artistic . . .

B No. You're no judge, Anna.

A But Wallace, I wonder . . .

B Yes?

A Which is the *front*, Wallace?

B Hah!

91 fv θð sz ʃ tʃ dʒ

A If I pay five each to both of you . . .

B Five each?

A Six if I can.

B Six isn't much, is it?

A I might manage a bit more.

B But this is a '*hush hush*' assignment!

A Ssshhh!

92 pb td kg tʃ dʒ fv θð sz ʃ mnŋ l

A One cup only, Mrs Lobb, I think . . . I diet, actually.

No bread, of course . . . Oh, that beautiful cake, if you like.

Not very big, I beg you . . . Oh, *too* much, I assure you. Well, that's not *too* large, I suppose . . . If I *have* to have a double portion please make the second slice small. Cream? On both – oh dear!

With even *more* cream? Really, this is excessive . . . I wish I could persuade you not to . . .

B Some jam on it?

A Nothing else.

B Ah.

A The jam will indeed be the *climax*!

93 r

A After all, you're only twenty-four, Ann.

B Mother, at twenty-four a girl's rather old.

A At *fifty*-four a girl's rather *older*, isn't she?

B But mother, I don't suppose father even *notices*.

A Father appreciates your mother 'as nature intended'!

B You're always nice. Where are you going, by the way?

A To my regular appointment with the hairdresser, if you want to know.

B For a shampoo?

A I have some grey hair, at the roots – which nature *never* intended!

94

A Do I have to do every question?

B You ought to try.

A How much time do I have?

B We give you about two hours.

A Two hours?

B Those who are quick can go early.

A And those who can't do it?

B *They* can go early *too,* I suppose.

A Good.

95

A My thigh and my arm still hurt. I expect to be up tomorrow, though.

Tea or coffee or something? The coffee isn't very good.

B Thanks. Tea, I think.

A Room Service? Could we have tea in Room Twenty, please? For two, please.

B I *am* sorry about the accident. We all miss you.

A Hm. I ought to learn to ski a bit better.

B Merely to *see* a bit better, Dick.

A I don't like to ski in glasses.

B If you can't see a *tree*, I think you should wear them.

96

A   That tree ought to go. We can't *see* anything for it.

B   Surely you don't want to destroy our ancient tree?

A   We can't *see* in here, and yet the sun's shining.

B   Anyway, I adore it.

A   I only say it spoils the view.

B   And that tree always reminds me of mother.

A   It's the *tree* I'm discussing. Don't bring your *mother* into it!

97

A   I expect you know Ian Green.

B   No, I don't know Ian Green.

A   Oh, I thought you *would*.

B   No, I don't.

A   I rather expected you *would*.

B   Why, I wonder? Is he influential?

A   His father is. Very influential: Magnus Green.

B   I know the *father*, of course.

A   I advise you to get to know the *son*.

B   Why all the hurry?

A   Mummy always knows best, dear.

98   ‿w‿   r   ‿j‿   pb td kg tʃ dʒ

A You're already a bit late. Where are you, anyway?

B Up at the club.

A Up at the club all this time?

B They had a match, actually. No point in rushing back, is there?
   I'll get a snack in the bar and stay on here with the boys for a bit.
   Celebrate our victory.

A That *Vickie* isn't in the bar, is she?

B Vickie? Who's Vickie? There's no one here except the boys.
   Oh, I see! *Behind* the bar! Mm, she *is* rather dishy, isn't she?

A Dishy, indeed! Be your age, Edwin!

B I *am* my age, darling.

A Watch it! Or I'll be over there in *no* time! Bye dear.

B Bye love . . . Anyway, what about you and that new *milkman*?

99   ⏝ r ⏝ fv θð sz ʃ

A   I wish I knew if you *are* or *aren't* coming with us.

B   I wish I knew myself if I am.

A   Surely the business isn't going to collapse if one of you goes out for a day, is it?

B   Of *course* it's not. But not *both* of us. If *I* go *out*, then *Willy* must stay *in*.

A   Why all the fuss about Willy? Willy's always out.

B   Willy's out *now*, actually. So it all depends on whether or not he returns, I'm sorry to say. I don't need to say any more, I suppose? Where are you off to?

A   I know where Willy is, I imagine. Though he may not know it, he's about to return in five minutes or less, is Willy. So be ready in five minutes.

B   Yes, Ada.

100   Revision

A   This dialogue appears again in almost identical form on the next page. But on the next page I've taken out all the links. What *you* are supposed to do is to practise a time or two from *this* page, and then turn over and do it without any help at all. Like to have a try at it?

B   I ought to have a try, I suppose.

[**100**]

A   This dialogue appears again in almost identical form on the previous page. But on *this* page I've taken out all the links. What *you* are supposed to do is to practise a time or two from *that* page, and then turn over and do it without any help at all. Like to have a try at it?

B   I've tried.

A   How did you do?

101 Conclusion

A   Well, anyway, I hope you'll continue to work on this very important aspect of the pronunciation of English, and that you've enjoyed the book. See you again, I hope.

B   (*Say anything you like here as long as you LINK IT UP appropriately!*)

Contractions

Introduction

Most students are aware that 'contractions' such as *they're, we've* and *he'd* represent, in writing or print, the usual spoken form of *they are, we have* and *he had* (or *he would*). Many students, however, are not sure how such contractions should be pronounced, or lack experience in pronouncing them. This section provides opportunity for the intensive practice of the main contracted forms encountered in written texts. It consists of short dialogues in which particular contractions are featured individually, in pairs, and in groups. The pronunciation of each contraction is indicated in phonemic transcription in the headings to the dialogues.

Linking contracted forms with following words

Particular care should be taken to link contracted forms smoothly and correctly with the word that immediately follows them. One pitfall to be avoided is that of 'over articulating', or exaggerating the pronunciation of a contraction at the junction with the next word. So, for example, some students tend to pronounce the *'d* in *he'd come* so deliberately that either a gap occurs between *he'd* and *come*, or the neutral vowel intrudes, resulting in *heeder come* /hiːdə ˈkʌm/.

DO

102   D'you /djuː/

A   Well, now, what exactly d'you have in mind?
B   What do I have in mind? Oh, yes. Yes. Well, d'you remember Partington?
A   Partington . . . Partington . . . Oh, *Partington*†! D'you mean the chap who . . . Hm! A dangerous man, Partington! Nasty man! Shocking!
B   D'you think he could do the job for us?
A   Perfectly. D'you want me to get him?

†Words in italics should be given extra emphasis.

DO

103   Don't /dəʊnt/

A   Don't open that, please.
B   Oh.
A   And please don't do that.
B   Don't do what?
A   That. If you don't mind.
B   And this?
A   Don't, please.
B   Don't, don't, don't! Don't you ever say 'do'? Well, I don't want to stay here any longer! I shall leave!
A   Do.

AM

104 I'm /aɪm/

A I'm lazy.
B I'm in love with you.
A I'm untidy.
B I'm in love with you.
A I'm extremely bad tempered.
B But I'm in *love* with you!
A And I'm in love with Michael.

IS

105 He's /hiːz/ John's /dʒɒnz/ Jack's /dʒæks/

A John's in, is he?
B He's out, actually.
A Oh. When's he expected back?
B No idea. Jack's in, though.
A Who's Jack?
B The boss.
A Surely, John's the boss. At least, he always *says* he's the boss – and, anyway, he's the man I want to see. But you say he's out?
B He *is* out.

IS

106 It's /ɪts/ Who's? /huːz/

A It's time! It's time to go!
B Oh, it's only half past. Plenty of time.
A Look, it's *awful* being late every time!
B Who's late?
A It's always the same! Late for everything! Late, late, late! It's ill-mannered! Discourteous!
B Relax.
A It's embarrassing!
B Relax!
A And they think it's *me*!!

IS

107 Isn't '/ɪznt/ It's /ɪts/ not
He's /hiːz/ not

A Wilfred, isn't that Mr Brown?
B Mr Brown? Here? Surely it's not Mr Brown.
A He isn't alone, either! Look!
B Well, that's certainly not *Mrs* Brown, is it?
A Isn't it Miss Middleton? Well, well!
B Good afternoon, Mr Brown.
A Isn't it a lovely day?

ARE ## i08 You're /jɔː(r)/†

A So you're Jane. Welcome.
B And you're Simon's father.
A So you're to be my daughter-in-law. Well, I must say you're *extremely* attractive. Beautiful, in fact.
B Thank you.
A But I have to confess you're just a little bit . . . well . . .
B Older than you expected?
A No, no, no, no. Er . . . did you meet my wife, by the way?
B Yes. And I must confess that . . . well . . .
A Simon's mother died, you know. I married again.

† Linking 'r' before a vowel. See Dialogue 93.

ARE

109 We're /wɪə(r)/

A Tell him we're here, will you?
B We're here. We're in here.
A Louder.
B We're in here, Mr Bagshaw! Please come along now! We're ready for you!
A Well, we're not going to wait all day. Where is he?
B In *there*, I think. If you see what I mean.

ARE

110 Aren't /ɑːnt/ —'re not

A You're not feeling tired, are you, dear?
B Only my legs, love. They aren't as young as they were!
A Well, we aren't far from the hotel now.
B We're not doing anything tonight, are we?
A Aren't we playing cards, dear? With the Potters?
B Oh, yes, of course.
A They're a splendid old couple, aren't they?
B Splendid, yes.
A Charming. And so dignified.
B Even so, we're not using *their* pack of cards again tonight, *I* can tell you!

WILL

111 I'll /aɪl/   You'll /juːl/

A I'll stop if you'll stop.
B If you'll stop, I'll stop, yes.
A You'll feel much better if you stop.
B Probably you'll lose your cough.
A And I'll certainly save money.
B I'll stop immediately, I think.
A Me too. I'll never have another.
B Or perhaps I'll have just *one* more.

WILL   **112** He'll /hiːl/   She'll /ʃiːl/

A   He'll open the gate for her.
B   She'll say thank you.
A   He'll walk up the path behind her.
B   She'll wait for him to open the door.
A   He'll look for his key.
B   She'll sniff at the roses till he finds it.
A   He'll say, 'Ah! Got it!'
B   She'll smile.
A   Here they come.
B   Sh!

WILL   **113** It'll /ɪtl/

A   It'll improve soon. The others'll be coming.
B   Then the fun'll begin, honestly.
A   John'll be bringing his guitar.
B   And Pete'll be here.
A   It'll warm up soon, honestly.
B   Don't go.
A   Please stay.
B   It'll be no fun without you.
A   It'll be *hopeless* without girls.

67

WILL **114** We'll /wiːl/ You'll /juːl/ They'll /ðeɪl/

A If you'll sign here, please . . .
B We'll do the rest.
A We'll arrange everything.
B We'll handle all the details.
A You'll have nothing more to worry about.
B You'll have no need to concern yourself any further.
A And those problems . . .
B Those anxieties . . .
A They'll all disappear – *dear* Mrs Parker . . .
B If you'll kindly sign here, please.
A Yes, here.

WILL **115** Won't /wəʊnt/

A He won't help us.
B He won't do anything.
A He won't cooperate.
B Why won't he help?
A Why won't he help us?
B Well, if he won't help us . . .
A If he won't, he won't.
B Right.
A But we won't forget, will we?
B We won't.

HAVE **116** I've /aɪv/ You've /juːv/

A I've got something for you.
B You've got something for me?
A Well, open it.
B A birthday present for me? Now what can it be?
A Like it?
B Thank you, darling. Just what I've always wanted. How did you guess?
A Darling, I've been thinking.
B Mm?
A You've got *so* many pipes now. How about a change next year?

HAVE **117** They've /ðeɪv/ We've /wiːv/

A We've failed.
B We've failed? Both of us?
A They've passed.
B They've passed? All of them?
A They've all passed except us.
B But if they've passed, how have we failed?
A Well, we *have*. I've seen the list.
B But we've planned a celebration!
A Forget it.
B We've bought all those bottles!
A Well, get them out, then.

HAVE **118** Haven't /'hævnt/ —'ve not

A I haven't always lived in this cottage, you know.
B Haven't you? How pretty it is!
A You've not been here long, of course.
B I haven't, no. Only a month, in fact. But it's a very nice village. I've grown to love it already.
A You haven't seen Ferringly House, yet, I suppose?
B Oh, it's magnificent! A beautiful house!
A But the *new* people haven't looked after it properly, you know.
B Well, I haven't seen it closely, of course, Mrs, er . . .
A Ferringly. Madeleine Ferringly.

HAVE **119** He's /hiːz/ She's /ʃiːz/ It's /ɪts/

A Jim's left, of course.
B He's left, too, has he?
A And Jean.
B Yes, she's gone to work at Fletcher's, they tell me.
A Oh, it's changed a lot since you were here. It's become much more efficient, of course. But it's lost the personal touch, I'm afraid.
B And what about our old friend Martin?
A Oh, Martin's stayed on.
B And become more efficient?
A He's had to. At avoiding work, that is.

HAVE **120** Hasn't /'hæznt/

A Hasn't the doctor come yet?
B No. The doctor hasn't been called.
A But this is urgent!
B Grandfather hasn't seen a doctor for sixty years.
  He's stubborn.
A Well tell him he *must*. He hasn't any choice.
B All right. But . . .
A And tell him Dr Fenton's a very good-looking young woman.

IS and HAS **121** —'s /s/ or /z/

A It's gone. It's not here.
B It's not there? Ask Vic where he's put it!
A Vic's gone.
B He's gone? Where's he gone?
A Nobody knows where he's gone.
B Well, get Sheila.
A Hm!
B Sheila too? But that's incredible!
A Is it?

HAD

122 He'd /hiːd/ You'd /juːd/

A He'd already gone when I got there.
B I wish you'd spoken to him.
A You really think he'd have helped?
B I think he'd have tried. I wish you'd seen him.
A Anyway, he'd left, as I say. He'd left early, actually.
B Oh.
A Perhaps he'd been told I was coming!

HAD

123 It'd /ɪtəd/

A Then we realised it'd escaped.
B It'd bitten through one of the bars and squeezed through the gap . . .
A And before it ran away . . .
B It'd been in the kitchen . . .
A It'd knocked everything over . . .
B Broken a dish, smashed a plate . . .
A And it'd eaten my supper!
B Anyway, thank you for bringing it back.
A We were afraid it'd been killed.
B And we missed it, *terribly*!

HAD

124 —'d /d/ Hadn't /ˈhædnt/

A He hadn't got time for a drink, he said . . .
B But when he'd drunk it . . .
A He said he hadn't got time for a meal . . .
B But when he'd eaten it . . .
A He said he hadn't come to stay the night . . .
B And when he'd stayed a week . . .
A He stayed another . . .
B And another . . .
A And hoped he hadn't outstayed his welcome.
B So, as I say – we'd *hoped* to let you have the spare room . . .
A If *he* hadn't come, and if . . . oh . . . er . . . hullo!
B Had a good day?

WOULD

125 I'd /aɪd/ You'd /juːd/ She'd /ʃiːd/

A If you'd like to know what I'd like, I'd like a car.
B She'd like a car, if you'd like to know.
A I'd *adore* some diamonds!
B She'd *adore* some diamonds!
A And I'd *love* a mink coat!
B Oh, she'd *love* a mink coat!
A But if that's too expensive . . .
B She'd like a hamburger.
A Oh, all right. I'll pay. One hamburger, please.
B Make it three.

WOULD **126** It'd /ɪtəd/

A   It'd be difficult to tell him, of course.
B   It'd obviously come as a shock.
A   It'd seem a bit harsh, I suppose.
B   Yes, I suppose it would.
A   And in a way, it'd be lonely without him.
B   Oh, it'd be quieter, no doubt.
A   But it'd be best to tell him.
B   Yes.
A   It'd be best if *you* told him.

WOULD **127** Wouldn't /'wʊdnt/

A   Well?
B   Well, they said they wouldn't paint it.
A   Wouldn't they put in new windows?
B   They wouldn't. Or repair the roof.
A   Or build a garage? Or modernise the kitchen?
B   No.
A   And the price?
B   They wouldn't lower it at all.
A   So you told them we wouldn't be interested, of course.
B   I told them we'd think about it.
A   Mm. Oh, dear. It's a lovely house, isn't it?
B   Mm. It wouldn't be a *bargain*, of course. But . . .

HAD and WOULD **128** —'d /d/

A   I knew you'd come.
B   You knew I *had* come? Or I *would* come?
A   Oh – *had* come, sorry. I was sure you *would* come, some time.
B   Well, how did you *know* I'd come?
A   I knew you'd come because I saw your car.
B   No, sorry – I mean how did you know I *would* come?
A   Well, it's obvious, isn't it? I'd told you Betty'd be here!

HAD and
WOULD

129 Hadn't /ˈhædnt/ Wouldn't /ˈwʊdnt/

A I hadn't expected a promotion.
B Well, you wouldn't, would you?
A I really hadn't expected it.
B You wouldn't, I suppose.
A I certainly wouldn't have got it if he'd checked my file.
B Oh, he checked it, certainly – because *I* gave it to him.
A But surely, if he'd seen that old letter, he wouldn't have promoted me.
B If he'd seen it, he wouldn't, no.
A Naughty girl.

MODALS
+HAVE

130 Could've /ˈkʊdəv/ etc.

A But, darling, if only you could've apologised!
B Hm! *He* should've apologised to *me*!
A But he's *older* than you. You could've said you were sorry, surely.
B I suppose I could've *said* I was. But that would've been telling a lie.
A But only a *little* one. You could've said it, just to keep the peace. For *my* sake!
B Oh, all right. You win. Where is the old devil?

131 Conclusion

A Well, that's the end of 'Contractions'.

B Mm.†

A Hope you've enjoyed it.

B Mm.

A Hope it's helped you.

B Mm.

A Hope we'll meet again some time.

B Mm.

> † On the tape, Speaker B's part is not recorded. Students should supply their own intonation on 'Mm' according to which of the many possible meanings they wish to convey.

Stress Time

Introduction

This section consists of dialogues in which the main rhythmical patterns of spoken English are presented first individually, then in pairs, then in larger combinations.

The rhythm of English

English is a 'stress-timed' language. That is to say the beats or *stress pulses* in connected speech follow each other at roughly equal intervals of time:

One	Two	Three	Four

This means that if there are any *unstressed syllables* between stresses, these have to be fitted in without delaying the regular beat of the stress pulses (printed in bold type throughout):

One		Two		Three		Four
One	and	Two	and	Three	and	Four
One	and a	Two	and a	Three	and a	Four
One	and then a	Two	and then a	Three	and then a	Four

The more unstressed syllables there are after a stress, the quicker they must be said in order to 'catch' the next pulse:

●	● .	● . .	● . . .	●
Yes,	**that** was	**pro**bably	**ne**cessary,	**John**

Sometimes a stress pulse is *silent* (indicated by ʌ)

●	●	ʌ	●
Yes	Yes	ʌ	Yes

76

This *silent stress* may sometimes be followed by some unstressed syllables:

●   ● ·   ∧ · · ·   ●
Yes,   **Peter,**   ∧ he was at   **home**

The silent stress can also come at the *beginning* of an utterance:

∧ · · · ●   ● ·
∧ He was at **home,**   **Peter**

After the basic unit of rhythm of the syllable comes the larger unit of the *foot*. A foot always begins with the stress pulse, in bold type, and takes in everything that comes after it up to the next stress. The foot boundary is indicated by an oblique stroke:

/**Yes,**	/**Peter,**	/∧ he was at	/ **home**
Foot 1	Foot 2	Foot 3	Foot 4

Presentation

Though variety in presentation is important, the following is a sequence of steps that has worked well as a standard procedure:

1. Students should listen to the recorded dialogue once or twice first.

2. Students should then answer comprehension questions and possibly re-tell the story to show that they understand it.

3. After this, students should listen again once or twice, and gently beat out the stresses – including silent stresses – either by tapping, or by beating the index finger on the open palm of the other hand.

4. They can next say and beat only the stressed syllables in the first line, keeping these at equal intervals:

    e.g.   /**Yes,** / **that**.../**pro**.../**ne**..., /**John**

5. Next, they can practise each foot separately, and then progressively in combination:

/**Yes**
/**that** was

/**Yes,** / **that** was

/**pro**bably
/**Yes,** / **that** was / **pro**bably

/**ne**cessary
/**Yes,** / **that** was / **pro**bably / **ne**cessary

/**John**
/**Yes,** / **that** was / **pro**bably / **ne**cessary, / **John**

6. Listen and repeat after the bleeps, beating time, using the paused version on the recording.

7. Say the whole dialogue tapping the beat, then without tapping, but with the teacher conducting the beat.

8. Perform the dialogue – possibly memorise it – aiming for perfection.

9. Old dialogues should be regularly revised.

Silent stress needs to be thought of and 'felt' as a beat. Students sometimes find it helpful to blow out their breath in a quick puff on the silent stress beat, or to make a sound such as 'Mm' wherever silent stress occurs:

/ ʌ he was at / **home**
(blow)
(Mm)

These devices help to maintain the beat. They also use up some breath and thereby perhaps assist the speaker to make any remaining syllables in the foot quick and light (students often find it hard not to put too much emphasis on unstressed syllables coming at the beginning of an utterance, after silent stress). Where there is a sequence of silent stresses it is probably best to count these out either aloud or in a whisper.

Rhythmical patterns and combinations

The contents list for this section (pages 99–100) specifies what foot pattern or patterns are featured in each dialogue. These patterns are also shown above each dialogue in the text. A large, heavy dot represents a stressed syllable and a small dot represents a non-stressed syllable. Dialogue 136, for instance, is devoted to the single foot pattern /●.. which means that it consists entirely of feet with a stressed syllable followed by two non-stressed syllables, e.g. / **fur**niture. Dialogue 143, on the other hand, features *three* foot types, namely /●, / ∧ and /●... This means that this dialogue is exclusively devoted to feet containing:

either a single stressed syllable only
or   silent stress
or   a stressed syllable followed by three non-stressed
     syllables, e.g. / **per**manently

It should be noted that the rhythmical specification for each dialogue indicates the types of feet used in that dialogue; it does not necessarily indicate the *order* in which they appear. Thus, for example, Dialogue 150 is devoted to the three foot types /●, /●.. and /●... *which can appear in any combination and in any order*.

132 / •

A   /Yes / Yes / Yes / Yes.
B   /No / No / No / No.
A   /Go! / Go!
B   /No / No.
A   /Yes! / Yes! / Yes! / Yes!
B   /No / No / No / No.
A   /Oh.

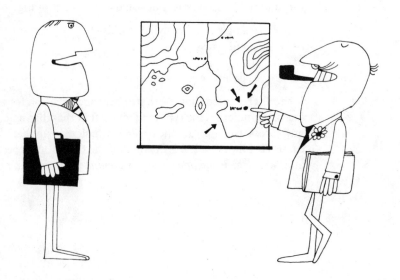

133 / • / ∧

A   /Where? / Where? / Where? / Where?
B   /There / There / There / There.
A   /When? / ∧ / When?
B   / ∧ / Now / ∧ / Now.
A   / ∧ / Who?
B   / ∧ / You.
A   / ∧ / Me?
B   / ∧ / ∧ / ∧ / You.

134 /•.

A /Jimmy! / Jimmy!
B / Jenny! / Jenny!
A /**Missed** you, / **Jimmy**!
B /**Missed** you, / **Jenny**!
A /**Like** me, / **Jimmy**?
B /**Love** you, / **Jenny**!

135 /•.

A /**Dinner's** / **rea**dy. / **Co**me and / **get** it.
B /**What's** for / **di**nner?
A /**Some**thing / **spe**cial.
B /**Some**thing / **spe**cial?
A /**Chi**cken / **cur**ry. / **Don't** you / **like** it?
B /**Yes,** I / **love** it. / **What's** for / **pu**dding?
A /**Wait** and / **see**.

136 /•..

A /**Thi**s is the / **fur**niture.
B /**Isn't** it / **terrible**?
A /**Terrible**?
B /**Terrible**.
A /**Thi**s is Aunt / **Agatha's** / **fur**niture, / **Mar**gery!
B /*She* doesn't / **need** it and / **neither** do / *we.*

137 / ● . . / ∧

A /When are you / bringing it?
B /Saturday, / probably.
A /Saturday.
B / ∧ / Probably. / ∧ / When can you / pay for it?
A /Saturday.
B / ∧ / ∧ / Saturday.
A / ∧ / Probably.
B / ∧ / ∧ / ∧ / Mm.

138 / ● . . .

A /Jonathan's an / irritating / fellow, but he's / necessary.
B /Irritating?
A /Irritating.
B /Necessary?
A /Necessary.
B /Certainly he's / *useful*, but I / wonder if he's / *necessary*?

139 / ● / ● .

A /One / single, / please.
B /One / single / where?
A /One / single / home.
B /Where's / home?
A /Where the / train / stops.
B /Twenty / pounds, / please.
A /Twenty / pounds! / Does it / only / stop / once?
B /Only / once. / Why?
A /Oh, / nothing.

140 /•/•..

A /Well, / Anthony, / **how** was the / **trip**?
B /**Fine**, / Valerie. / **Fine**.
A /**Good**.
B /**Valerie**, / **when** did you / **buy** that new –
A /**How** do you / **like** it, my / **love**?
B /**Where** did you / **buy** it my / **love**?
A /**Anthony**. / **That's** what I / **wanted** to / **tell** you a/**bout**.
B /**What** did it / **cost** me, my / **sweet**?

141 /•/∧/•..

A /**Now**, / Julia. / **Listen** to / **me**!
B /**Yes**, Uncle / Willy, of / *course*.
A / ∧ /**Julia** –
B /**Yes**?
A /**Oh**! / **This** is a / **difficult** / **thing** to dis/**cuss**!
B /**Why** should you / **want** to dis/**cuss** it at / **all**?
A /**Why**?
B /**Yes**. / ∧ / **Why** don't you / **buy** me a / **whisky** in/**stead**?

142 / • / • . . .

A /Vegetables?
B /No / vegetables, / **please.**
A /No / vegetables.
B /**Just** / **chicken** and a / **little** of the / **pudding** over / **there.**
A /**Separately.**
B /No.
A /**Pud**ding with the / **meat**?
B /**Naturally.**
A /**Certainly, Ma**/**dame.**

143 / • / ∧ / • . . .

A /**Pen**dlebury's / coming in a / minute if he / **can.**
B /**Coming** in a / **minute** if he / *can*!
A / ∧ / **Pen**dlebury / **seems** to be en/**gaged.**
B /**Tell** / **Pendlebury**, / ∧ / **tell** him from his / **boss**, / ∧ / **tell** him that he's / **fired**!
A /**Per**manently?
B /**Per**manently, / **defi**nitely, / **pos**itively / **fired**!
A /**Poor** / **Pen**dlebury.
B /**Hah**!

144 / • . / ∧ / • . .

A /This is a / **ques**tion for / **Doc**tor / **Carr**ington.

B /**What's** the / **ques**tion?

A / ∧ / **Here's** the / **ques**tion. / ∧ / ∧ / **Let's** i/**ma**gine that / *you* are the /**on**ly / **per**son / **left** in the / **world** ex/**cept** for / **one** other / **per**son.

B / ∧ / **Splen**did. / ∧ / **In**teresting / **ques**tion.

A /**Who** would you / **choose**, Doctor / **Carr**ington?

B / ∧ / ∧ / ∧ / ∧ / **Is** my / **wife** in the / **au**dience?

145 / • . / • . . .

A /**Come** and / **see** us at our / **new** a/**part**ment.

B /**Where's** your / **new** a/**part**ment? / Is it in a/**no**ther / **dis**trict?

A /**No**, it's / **very** / **close** to the a/**part**ment that I / **used** to / **live** in. /**Come** and / **see** us.

B /**How** about to/**mo**rrow?

A /**Round** about / **se**ven? We're at / **home** by / **se**ven. / **Come** and have some / **di**nner with us, / **Ja**net.

B /**John**, you / **ha**ven't / **ac**tually / **told** me / **yet** who / '**us**' is!

146 / • . / ∧ / • . . .

A /Is it / ∧ / **Ja**nuary?
B /**No**, it's / **Feb**ruary.
A / ∧ / Is it / ∧ / **Mon**day?
B /**No**, it's / **Tues**day.
A /**Is** it / ∧ / **morn**ing?
B /**No**, the / **mid**dle of the / **after**/**noon**, and it'll / **soon** be / **time** for an
   im/**port**ant / visitor to / **come** and / **see** you – your / **wife** is / **com**ing.
A / ∧ / ∧ / **Bet**ty. / ∧ / ∧ / **That's** her / **na**me – it's / *Betty*.
B / ∧ / **Erm**...

147 / • . . / • . . .

A /**Why** was he / **try**ing to em/**barr**ass me?
B /**Prob**ably he / **wan**ted you to / **no**tice him.
A /**Why** was he / **rude** to me?
B /**Prob**ably he's / **plan**ning to / **marry** you.
A /**Why** is he / **tal**king to that / **stu**pid little / **Al**ison?
B /**Why** are you / **let**ting him?

148 /•../∧/•...

A /Certainly. / ∧ / Definitely. / ∧ / ∧ / Definitely. / ∧ / ∧ / Ready by
/January, / definitely. / ∧ / ∧ / Terribly / sorry a/bout the de/lay, but
I / promise de/livery in / January. / ∧ / ∧ / Thank you for / waiting
so/patiently.

B / ∧ / ∧ / ∧ / Why did you / tell him you'll de/liver in / January?
/ ∧ / Probably it / won't be com/pleted by / February.

A /Probably it / won't be com/pleted at / all.

149 /•/∧/•./•..

A /One, / two, / three, / four / men.
B / ∧ / Thirteen, / fourteen, / fifteen, / sixteen / women.
A / ∧ / One / man to / four / women.
B / ∧ / Four / women to / one / man.
A / ∧ / Splendid i/dea!
B / ∧ / Hm! / ∧ / Terrible!

150 /•/•../•...

A /Mike, / how shall I / send it to you?
B /Give it to Y/vonne.
A /Is she re/liable?
B /Perfectly re/liable – she'll / give it to me.
A /After she's / read it I sup/pose!

151 / • / ∧ / • .. / • ...

A /Yes. / ∧ / Certainly. / ∧ / Definitely.

B / ∧ / ∧ / ∧ / Ben... / ∧ / Isn't it a / **fact** that you / **say**, / 'Certainly',
   / ∧ / 'Definitely' / ∧ / **each** time you / **talk** to a / **cus**tomer?

A / ∧ / ∧ / **Po**ssibly, / **dear**.

B /Definitely, / **dear**.

152 / • / • . / • .. / • ...

A /Well, / Sammy, / **when** will you / **do** it for me?

B /Will to/**morrow** / **do**?

A /Yes, to/**morrow** will be / **ad**mirable.

B /**When** do I / **get** my / **money**?

A /**When** you've / **done** it, / **Sa**mmy.

B /**How** do I / **know** I'll / **get** it?

A /**How** will I / **know** you've / **done** it? / **You** and / **I** must / **trust** each
   /other, / **Sa**mmy.

B /Mm. / Yes. / Yes, I sup/**pose** there's / **no** al/**ter**native.

153 /•/∧/•./•../•...

A   /Oh! / ∧ / Martin! / ∧ / Marvellous! / ∧ / Give it to me!
B   / ∧ / Isn't it a / lovely / animal? / ∧ / Careful, it'll / bite!
A   /No, it / won't / bite me, it / knows I / love it al/ready.
B   /Yes, it / seems to / like you.
A   /Does it / like / *you*?
B   / ∧ / Possibly. / ∧ / Certainly it / likes my / *fingers*!
A   / ∧ / ∧ / ∧ / ∧ / Ouch!

154 /∧./•

A   / ∧ He/llo?
B   / ∧ Y/vonne? / ∧ It's / Mike. / ∧ I'm / back. / ∧ / ∧ / ∧ Is / Sam /there?
A   /No, / Mike. / ∧ / ∧ There's / just / me.
B   / ∧ / ∧ I / don't / trust / Sam. / ∧ O./K.?
A   / ∧ O./K. / ∧ Good/bye, / Mike. / ∧ / ∧ / ∧ / ∧ Sam! / ∧ / Sam! / ∧ / ∧ / ∧ It's /Mike! / ∧ / ∧ / ∧ He's / back!

155 / ʌ../•

A / ʌ Is it / **there**?
B / ʌ Is it / **where**?
A / ʌ On the / **chair**.
B / ʌ On the / **chair**?
A / ʌ By the / **door**.
B / ʌ By the / **door**?
A / ʌ On the / **floor**.
B / ʌ On the / **floor**?
A / ʌ On the / **bed**.
B / ʌ / ʌ / ʌ On your / **head**!

156 / ʌ./•.

A / ʌ It's / **winning**! / ʌ / ʌ It's / **winning**!! / ʌ It's / **winning**, / **Willy**!
B / ʌ / ʌ The / **winner**! / ʌ The / **winner**!!! / ʌ / ʌ Ter/**rific**!!!
A / ʌ / ʌ / ʌ / ʌ / ʌ / ʌ / ʌ It's / **won** me – / ʌ / ʌ / It's / **won** me –
/ ʌ / ʌ / It's / **won** me – / ʌ a / **hun**dred / **do**llars!
B / ʌ It's / **won** me – / ʌ / ʌ a /*thousand* / **do**llars!
A / ʌ A / **thou**sand? / ʌ But / **didn**'t you / **bet** the / **same** a/**mount** as
/*me*?
B / ʌ I / **didn**'t.
A / ʌ / **Oh**.

157 / ʌ../•.

A / ʌ There's a / **woman**. / ʌ In my / **office**. / ʌ And she / **says** she
/**wants** to / **see** you.
B / ʌ But I'm / **bu**sy.
A / ʌ Well she / **says** she / **wants** to / **see** you.
B / ʌ But I'm / **bu**sy!
A / ʌ But she's / **sure** you'll / **want** to / **see** her.
B / ʌ Is she / **pretty**?
A / ʌ In a / **sort** of / **way** she's / **pretty**. / ʌ But you're / **bu**sy.
B / ʌ In a / **sort** of / **way**, I'm / **bu**sy. / ʌ But per/**haps** I / **ought** to . . .

158 / ∧ . . . / ● .

A   / ∧ I was at / Jonah's. / ∧ We had a / **par**ty.

B   / ∧ You had a / **par**ty.

A   / ∧ It was / **love**ly. / ∧ It was a / **love**ly / **par**ty. / ∧ There was a /**love**ly / **crow**d of / **peo**ple. / ∧ It was a / **love**ly / **par**ty. / ∧ But I'm a / **lit**tle / **late** for –

B   / ∧ It's in the / **o**ven. / ∧ It was ex/**treme**ly / **nice** at / **sev**en. / ∧ But at e/**lev**en –

A   / ∧ It'll be / **love**ly, / **dar**ling. / ∧ It'll be / **love**ly.

159 / ∧ . / ● . .

A   / ∧ It's / **pro**bably / **some**one for / **Dor**othy.

B   / ∧ He's / **knock**ing a/**gain**, Mrs / **Wel**lington. / ∧ I'll / **o**pen the /**cur**tains and / **see** who it – / ∧ Po/**lice**! The po/**lice**! Mrs / **Wel**lington! / ∧ We / **ha**ven't done / **an**ything / **wrong**, Mrs / **Wel**lington. / ∧ They've / **pro**bably / **ma**de a mis/**take**, and we / **ought** to in/**form** them that – / ∧ / ∧ / ∧ Well, / **where** have you / *gone*, Mrs /**Wel**lington?

160 / ∧ . . . / ● . .

A   / ∧ He was a / **won**derful / **trea**surer.

B   / ∧ He was a / **mar**vellous / **trea**surer.

A   / ∧ He was con/**sid**erate.

B   / ∧ He was a / *gentleman*.

A   / ∧ And he was / **hu**morous.

B   / ∧ He was a / **com**ical / **fel**low, and / **none** of us / ever sus/**pec**ted that / **some**thing pe/**cu**liar was / **hap**pening.

A   / ∧ And that the / **joke** was on / *us*!

161 / ∧ .. / ● ...

A / ∧ Is there / **sugar** in it ?

B / ∧ You pre/**fer** it with / **sugar** in it.

A / ∧ Yes, I / **u**sually / **do**, but it's / **re**cently been / **ma**king me a / **bit** /**sick**.

B / ∧ Are you / **com**fortable ?

A /**Rea**sonably.

B / ∧ Do you / **think** it'll be / **born** on the e/**le**venth, as you / **said** ?

A / ∧ He'll be / **born** on the e/**le**venth at e/***le***ven, as I / **said**. / ∧ / **Punc**tually!

162 / ∧ . / ● / ∧ . / ● .

A / ∧ You /**did**!

B / ∧ I / **did**n't!

A / ∧ You / **did**!

B / ∧ I / **did**n't!

A / ∧ You / **did**! / ∧ You / **did**!

B /**No**, I / **did**n't!

A / ∧ / **Ouch**! / ∧ You / **hit** me!

B / ∧ / ∧ I / **did**!

163 / ∧ . / ● / ● .

A / ∧ He's / **quite** / **hand**some.

B / ∧ I / **think** he's / **ug**ly.

A / ∧ He's / **ra**ther / **clev**er.

B / ∧ He's / **vain**. / ∧ Con/**ceit**ed.

A / ∧ He's / **rich**.

B / ∧ He / **knows** it!

A / ∧ / ∧ / ∧ He / **thinks** you're / **pret**ty.

B / ∧ / ∧ He / **did**n't / ***say*** that.

A / ∧ / ∧ He / **did**.

164 / ʌ . / • / ʌ . . / • / • .

A / ʌ Some / **eggs**, / ʌ and a / **small** / **ca**bbage.

B / ʌ A / **small** / **ca**bbage. / ʌ And the / **eggs**?
/ ʌ A / **do**zen?

A / ʌ Are they / **fresh**?

B / ʌ Are they / **fresh**? / ʌ / ʌ Of / **course** they're / **fresh**.

A / ʌ The / **last** / **eggs** I / **bought**, / ʌ / ʌ they were/ **bad**.

B / ʌ Did you / **buy** them / **here**?

A / ʌ I / **don't** re/**mem**ber. / ʌ / ʌ Per/**haps** I / **did**. / ʌ / ʌ Per/**haps** I
/**did**n't.

B / ʌ / ʌ / **Take** / *half* a / **do**zen, / **then**.

165 / ∧ . / ● . / ∧ . . / ● . . / .

A / ∧ On / **Mon**day, / ∧ you were / **going** to / **men**d it.

B / ∧ I / **couldn**'t, / ∧ I was / **busy** on / **Mon**day.

A / ∧ Well, / **Peter**, / ∧ will you / **do** it this / **evening**?

B / ∧ I'm / **sorry**, / ∧ but I'm / **off** to a / **meeting**. / ∧ I /**pro**mise you, / ∧ I'll re/**pair** it to/**morrow**. / **Where** are you / **going**?

A / ∧ For the / **tools**.

B / **Why**?

A / ∧ For/**get** it. / ∧ / ∧ I'll re/**pair** it my/**self**.

166 / ∧ . / ● . / ∧ . . / ● . . / ● . . .

A / ∧ The / **smell** of it! / ∧ It's the / **smell** of it, / **Gla**dys!

B / ∧ But it's / *nice* if you / **taste** it.

A / ∧ It's the / **smell** of it!

B / ∧ It's / **mar**vellous. / ∧ It's a / **won**derful / **fla**vour. / ∧ / ∧ It was / **ra**ther ex/**pen**sive, / **Char**lie.

A / ∧ You can / **eat** it / **for** me, / **can**'t you?

B / ∧ I sup/**pose** I can / **eat** it.

A / ∧ Well en/**joy** it. / ∧ And I'll / **meet** you out/**side**.

167 / ∧ . . / ● / ∧ . . . / ● .

A / ∧ It's a / **boy**. / ∧ And it's a / **big** one.

B / ∧ And my / **wife**?

A / ∧ She was a / **mar**vel. / ∧ And she's / **fine**.

B / ∧ Can I / **see** her?

A / ∧ You can / **see** them / **both** at about / **six**.

B / ∧ Well, I'm ex/**treme**ly / **grate**ful, / **Sis**ter. / ∧ And I'll / **see** you /**la**ter. / ∧ / ∧ / ∧ / ∧ I'm a / **fa**ther! / ∧ And it's a / **boy**! / ∧ I must /**do** some /**shop**ping / **quick**ly. / ∧ I must / **buy** some / **flow**ers. / ∧ / ∧ And a / **train**.

168 / ʌ .. / ● .. / ʌ ... / ● ...

A   / ʌ And you're / **fond** of him?

B   / ʌ Well, I'm in / **love** with him.

A   / ʌ You were in / **love** with the /**architect**. / ʌ And the so/**licitor**.
/ ʌ And the / **fellow** with the / **wife** and the in/**numerable** / **children**.

B   / ʌ But / **this** is / **different**, I can / **promise** you.

A   / ʌ And they were / **hopeless** at / **golf**, I re/**member**.

B   / ʌ He's the / **regional** / **champion**.

A   / ʌ / ʌ You see you / **never** have a / **sense** of pro/*portion*, / **Marilyn**.

Detailed list of contents

Clusters

Contractions

Stress Time